# VIRTUOUS CYCLE
# ECONOMICS

This book is a guideline on how to make today's economy work for you and how to create upward mobility in a flat or stagnated middle class.

# VIRTUOUS CYCLE ECONOMICS

### The Soldier's Guidebook

## Kory T. Morris

COPYRIGHT © 2014 BY KORY T. MORRIS.

LIBRARY OF CONGRESS CONTROL NUMBER: 2014913925
| ISBN: | HARDCOVER | 978-1-4990-5805-5 |
| | SOFTCOVER | 978-1-4990-5806-2 |
| | EBOOK | 978-1-4990-5807-9 |

All rights reserved. No part of this book may be reproduced or transmitted in any form or by any means, electronic or mechanical, including photocopying, recording, or by any information storage and retrieval system, without permission in writing from the copyright owner.

Any people depicted in stock imagery provided by Thinkstock are models, and such images are being used for illustrative purposes only.
Certain stock imagery © Thinkstock.

This book was printed in the United States of America.

Rev. date: 08/01/2014

To order additional copies of this book, contact:
Xlibris LLC
1-888-795-4274
www.Xlibris.com
Orders@Xlibris.com
662022

# CONTENTS

- ✓ Acknowledgments ................................................................. 7
- ✓ Synopsis ................................................................................. 9

- ✓ The Economy Past and Present ............................................ 11
- ✓ Credit (The Good, the Bad, and the Ugly) .......................... 19
- ✓ The Bad ................................................................................ 21
- ✓ The Ugly ............................................................................... 24
- ✓ How to Live in Excess and Afford It .................................... 27
- ✓ Your Security Clearance and Your Finances ....................... 32
- ✓ Cash Only? ........................................................................... 34
- ✓ Budgeting ............................................................................. 37
- ✓ Investing for Beginners ........................................................ 40
- ✓ Wealth Management ............................................................ 48

- ✓ About the Author ................................................................. 51

# Acknowledgments

I am most grateful to *God*, who has shown me favor and has changed my life for the better. He has set me on the right path and has been guiding my hand with every stroke of my keyboard.

Thanks to Heather Morris, my wife of seven years who has been patient with me throughout our relationship's ups and downs. I am very happy that she is here now to enjoy the fruits of our labor.

Thanks to my brother, Freddie Greg Morris, who has been instrumental in making this endeavor a success, and who has always encouraged me even when my goals seem too lofty to achieve.

I would also like to thank my high-school soccer coach, Tom Blauvelt, for believing in me and demonstrating to me while still in my youth that there were still good people that did good deeds for the sake of being good.

Thanks to my aunt and uncle, Jennief and Godfrey Watson, who made it possible for us to migrate to the United States from Jamaica and altered the course of our lives forever.

Thank you to my father, Frederick Morris, who has been an inspiration to me since childhood, and who has demonstrated through his deeds and his love that anything is possible if you put your heart and soul into something you believe in.

Thank you to my mother, Lorna Morris, who gave me the tools necessary to be where I am today, and who loved me in spite of my faults and failures as a son. She is a beacon of kindness and compassion and puts the needs of others above her own.

# Synopsis

This book is intended to be an easily read and understood guideline that is intended on giving the reader a brief overview of our economy. This covers past and present situations, occurrences, and fundamentals of our capitalistic society and is intended to reveal flaws, fixes, and methods of coping with the status quo.

The book also contains a breakdown of how the current credit system became what it is today, its benefits, its shortcomings, and how to cope and begin to take advantage of strategies that can be beneficial to the middle-class citizen. It also covers the importance of having good credit and why the credit bureaus have little to no incentive to keep an accurate record of your FICO score. It also explains how we are viewed in the eyes of our creditors in terms of our risk tolerance levels and steps that can be taken to correct and monitor your credit score with no out of pocket cost to the consumer.

Also included are tips on how to live above the means of one's salary through the year by averaging one's tax returns over a period of time prescribed in the book. This is intended to allow the reader to accurately predict a rate of tax return (assuming the conditions are as set forth in the book) and allow for a monthly additional budget utilizing a credit card. This utilization of the card will account for the interest that will be accrued and first subtracted from the tax return amount. That amount will then be divided by twelve to give the resulting sum of the monthly additional spending allowed above one's monthly salary.

An attempt has also been made to explain the interconnectivity of one's security clearance and perceived level of risk when an individual is carrying a large amount of debt. It illustrates how one's security clearance may be taken away due to issues with debt and provides advice on steps that may be taken to stop or delay this process through bankruptcy.

The book explains what to expect after filing bankruptcy, and gives a strategy or method of what to do while going through the process and emerging more financially stable. A plan of action for constructing a functional budget is explained and illustrated, and a guide for investing the newly available capital is outlined for the beginner level investor.

An attempt to close the cycle is done by explaining what to do with new found wealth if you are successful in your endeavors in the form of wealth management and tax advice.

# The Economy Past and Present

Our economy is the greatest economy the world has ever seen, and we have one of the most profitable business models in the history of the world called capitalism.

In this system of capitalism, we are in what is called a free market or a free economy. The reason it is called a free market or a free economy is that the businesses are given more control to make their own decisions. The foundation of this system is based upon having the least amount of government interference possible. A core belief within this system that has held true is that in a free market, competition drives innovation.

Even though we are called a free market, no market is truly free. The government still sets the parameters (rules) by which the free market operates and determines what the consequences are for breaking these sets of rules.

In 1913, for example, the income tax was established with the goal of having a pool of money available to accomplish the things together for the good of the country that we could not accomplish individually. These were things such as road maintenance, infrastructure development, public transportation, education, and so on.

**KORY T. MORRIS**

In the years when the country flourished, the income tax was 91% on the wealthiest 1% of Americans and has been kept at 70% for the most part until the late 1970s. Around 1978, when the tax rate began to decrease for the wealthiest 1%, the economy made a drastic shift towards benefitting the top 1%. The other 99% of Americans that made up the middle class and the poor started to see their wages stagnate (stay the same) or even decline.

As a result of this change in the tax rate, the income disparity (gap) between a CEO (chief executive officer) and the average worker began to widen. In 1970, the average income for an average male worker was about $48,000 (adjusting for inflation and purchasing power), while the average income for a CEO of a large corporation in the same time period was about $375,000. By late 1978, the income of the average male worker had been reduced or stayed the same in the interest of corporate profits.

This created a balloon effect where the income of the wealthiest Americans went up to about $1.2 million, while the income of the middle class and the poor stagnated (stayed the same) or, in most cases, declined to approximately $37,500 (adjusting for inflation and purchasing power). As a result, the 1% had to invent new ways of solving the problem of inflation in the absence of a wage increase for the other 99% of Americans.

Their answer was to promote women being in the workforce and taking on full-time jobs outside of the home. This gave rise to the traditional two-income families we see today in the United States and around the world.

To allow for this social change to occur without much outcry (complaining) from the American public, popular artists and Hollywood were used to promote this new concept. Popular artists like Dolly Parton who sang the hit song "9 to 5" in 1980 were used to promote what was to be the new normal, and women were placed in movie roles that showed them being happy in the workplace—which inspired women to dream big. Inspirational movies depicted women as CEOs (chief executive officers) of companies breaking through the glass ceiling (a belief by women that certain jobs are only available to men in the workplace and equal work doesn't result in equal pay for women).

As a result of this social change, both husband and wife in a household working nine-to-five jobs became acceptable and a necessary staple in our society. Working longer hours for stagnating wages became the normal way of life, and the pay of the average middle-class American worker did not adjust for inflation. As a result, inflation again caught up to this new dynamic of the two-income household, and an increase in the minimum wage was again knocking on the front door of companies and corporations.

Companies now had to seek out new ways to keep maintaining their growth rate and show increasing profits to shareholders (people that have purchased stock or a piece of the company through a private entity or the stock market). Instead of raising the minimum wage, a new concept of allowing families to maintain their standard of living on less than the required income as the cost of goods and services rose was introduced. This new concept was the credit card. This became the new widely accepted artificial means of propping up the middle class without actually having to raise the minimum wage.

This new means of supplementing your income now allowed average Americans to live out their lives with all the comforts they were used to having without really being able to afford it on their current salaries. This again bought the wealthiest 1% and the corporations a few more years to artificially keep wages low and profits high without much outcry (complaining) from the middle-class workforce.

However, this too had to come to an end as credit-card interest rates were getting higher and the credit card users were reaching and exceeding their credit limits by living above their means.

To solve this crisis, the companies and corporations did not raise the minimum wage; but instead, they introduced the concept of tapping into your home's value known as the equity (the difference between the current value of your home and what you still owe the bank or financial institution that provided the loan to purchase the property) as a form of obtaining more credit.

This temporary fix again lasted for a few years. However, after middle-class Americans began using their homes' equity to pay off credit card debt, buy that new car they always wanted, go on dream vacations, and much more, inflation again caught up to the stagnated wages.

This artificial means of propping up the economy in the absence of a minimum wage increase would become responsible for the stock market crash and economic downturn of the 2007–2008 era and would cause a financial crisis that rivaled that of the Great Depression (1929–1939).

As a result of wages being stagnated (no movement) for the last thirty years (when adjusting for inflation), the middle class did not have enough purchasing power to sustain real growth. The only growth occurs at the top 1% as the debt being accrued by the middle class is financed by the 1% and is spent on products being produced by companies owned by the top 1% of the population. The growth, therefore, becomes artificial for the rest of the country (the other 99%).

Seventy percent (70%) of our free-market economy is powered by consumer spending. There are roughly three hundred million

## VIRTUOUS CYCLE ECONOMICS

Americans of which only four hundred fit into the category of the top 1%. These people are identified as those who make over $380,000 per year on the low end, $3 million per year at the median (middle) level, and over $10 million per year on the high end. The top 1% possesses over half of the entire country's wealth. This means every person in that group of four hundred earns approximately $375,000 per person for the 150 million people they account for in wealth.

The parameters for determining if you are a middle-class American is $50,000 give or take 50% on the high and low end. This means if you make between $25,000 and $75,000 per year, you are considered to be a middle-class citizen.

If the middle-class wages are not sufficient (enough), then there is less discretionary spending (spending money on things that you only want but don't necessarily need). If there is less discretionary spending combined with the fear of an uncertain financial future, the economy cannot perform as intended.

This creates an imbalance in the free economy system since there is no longer anyone to consume the goods and services produced as the middle class is reduced to buying only the necessities. Contrary to popular belief, millionaires are not the "job creators." The middle-class workers create the jobs when they consume goods, which create demand in a particular sector (area). Four hundred people at the top (1%) can only consume so many goods and services. They can only eat a few times a day, they can only drive so many cars, they can only have so many houses, and they can only get a haircut so many times per year.

This can be illustrated by a simple example of how to look at how the economy is powered by the middle class. If you own a restaurant and five millionaires came in every day to eat. They order the most expensive meal on the menu and spend $200 on food and beverages, which is much higher than the average spent per person today. The five millionaires even leave a tip of $50 each for the wait staff. This would mean you made $1,000 on food and beverages and $250 in tips for the wait staff. However, how often are those five millionaires going to come into your restaurant if you own, say, an Olive Garden, Hooters, Buffalo Wild Wings, or TGI Fridays?

On the other hand, the average restaurant sees traffic of over two hundred average customers per day. If each customer spends $10 to $15 and tip the wait staff only $2 each, your company would be doing a lot better. This would mean you would make between $2,000 to $3,000 on your food and beverages, and your wait staff would make $400 in tips. The odds of ordinary middle-class Americans showing up at your place of business are much higher than millionaires doing so.

The top 1% keeps their money in the stock market, mutual funds, bonds, natural resources, raw materials, precious metals, art, in a trust, or investments to make more money. They do nothing to enhance the human condition as it refers to the middle class. The rich only create jobs as a byproduct (unintended result) of trying to get richer and would choose to use other means of obtaining the labor needed to produce their goods and services without helping the middle class by creating any jobs whatsoever.

This can be seen by taking a closer look at some of the most profitable companies like Google, Johnson & Johnson, and Amazon. These companies are making record profits but are cutting jobs. This is because in the interest of keeping the shareholders happy and showing growth in revenue each quarter (the year is divided into three month increments), the companies find ways to cut costs.

In the case of Amazon, they have streamlined the process so much with automated systems that they only need sixty thousand workers for what used to require one million workers. This means that Amazon—through innovation driven by a need to show more profitability—has put 940,000 workers out of work who had good-paying jobs prior to this shift to automated production.

This is the trend that has led to the massive cuts in employment across the United States. There are often talks of bringing back good factory work or production-oriented jobs such as making cars or working on machinery that have migrated overseas. However, this is a misguided notion (belief) by the general population. It is not the Chinese or Japan who is primarily responsible for us losing these production-oriented jobs; it is the evolution of technology and the world becoming a global market. Take the iPhone for example, which is one of today's highest-selling cell phones. The iPhone is a globally constructed product which has 34% of it made in Japan, 17% made in Germany, 13% made in South Korea, 6% in the United States, 3.6% in China, and 26.4% in other developing nations. These are leaps in technology and steps that have been taken that cannot be undone.

A robot now works on that assembly line, and a robot fixes that robot now when it is not operating at peak performance and can tell within a millisecond when that other robot is malfunctioning. These are things that we, as humans, are not able to accomplish with the efficiency of a machine. Keep in mind that the robot doesn't need sleep, breaks for food, can work twenty-four hours per day, requires no wages, and only needs to be supervised by one or two technicians to ensure everything runs smoothly. How can we get those jobs back? The answer is we cannot.

The economic makeup of the world has evolved, and we need to evolve with it—or we will not be at the top for long as a nation. Americans will still have the richest people in the world, but that will only be accounted for by the wealthiest 1% (four hundred people). In other words if the other 99% of Americans were dirt-poor, we would still be considered rich because of the amount of money being accrued at the top by the richest four hundred people in our nation.

This is the reason there should be a push to educate our young Americans in order to give them a chance to succeed in this global economy as we are no longer just competing against our classmates or the rest of the kids in our school, state, or country. We are now competing with that other kid sitting at his or her desk anywhere else in the world. The sooner we realize this change, the sooner we can start changing our way of thinking, provide common-sense solutions for the way ahead, and look to the future.

This passage was in no way intended to incite class warfare, resentment toward the rich who either worked hard themselves or had parents or grandparents who worked extremely hard to get where they are today, or to incite hatred toward our government. It was intended to educate the reader on the history of our economy in the past and show us where we are today with the intent and hope of shaping a better future for all.

# Credit (The Good, the Bad, and the Ugly)

Your credit is a direct reflection of you in the eyes of most businesses. Your credit score is used by many entities to make decisions about allowing you to receive everything from goods and services to your potential for employment.

Most job applications today will include a credit check through one of the three major credit bureaus (Experian, Trans Union, or Equifax). These institutions have been given the authority to monitor all the financial and social activities of every American citizen. They monitor your job status, your place of residence, your age and race demographic information, financial difficulty, and your overall financial risk as a borrower or consumer.

This can be a good thing if your information is correct and up to date 100% of the time. However, if you have any negative information such as a late payment, bankruptcy, high credit card debt or consumer debt, or too many inquiries (applications for loans or credit cards), your credit score may work against you.

The scoring of credit ranges from 300 to 850 with each number associated with a category of risk. Any score below 600–619 will make it difficult to obtain a loan or credit card. If you do obtain a loan or credit card with this credit score range, you can expect to get a higher rate of interest than a person with a higher credit rating. Good credit starts at around the 660 to the 700 score range. Anything above 700 will usually get you good terms and a lower rate of interest.

## The Bad

Having a bad credit rating can affect everything from your cable and utilities to your suitability for employment. If you are in the military or you are a government employee, this may also affect your ability to obtain or keep your security clearance.

If your apply for cable or try to get your lights and water turned on after buying a new home and your credit rating is in the lower range (below a score of 619) you may be required to pay a down payment or a security deposit before you are offered service.

As a consumer, you have the right to check your credit once per year for free from each of the credit bureaus. The best way to keep track of your credit for free is to obtain one report from each credit bureau every four months. For example, get your Trans Union report in the first four months, your Experian in the next four months, and then your Equifax for the last four months. The reason for getting the Equifax last is they usually have the most inaccurate information, so they usually display the lowest credit score.

By using this method you will be able to track your credit throughout the year in increments without paying for your report. There are also other services that offer free credit report monitoring such as a Capital One Quick Silver card and many other internet monitoring services. However, as we know, nothing in life is usually free unless mandated by the government when it comes to companies. These companies offering to monitor your credit for free are obtaining your information and selling it to third parties as a means of obtaining revenue (money).

They offer you the service for free and in the small print of the contract you give them permission to handle your information however they see fit. This is where they make their money. A third party, such as Wal-Mart, may purchase that information to target their advertising toward you in an e-mail, in conventional mail offers, or by offering sales specific to the items that you are predisposed (things you like to buy) to purchasing based on your purchasing history.

Have you ever googled something online and, within a few hours, the same product you google is now in your e-mail inbox saying "Items we found for you?" This is because your information is being traded, bought, and sold. Amazon, Wal-Mart, eBay, and many other corporations use these methods of targeted marketing and receive the majority of their information from outlets like Facebook, Twitter, YouTube, Yahoo, and many others.

When we sign up for Facebook for example, we willingly put all our information out there with photos (which tells them your race), fill out our date of birth (gives age demographic information), add friends and family members (which gives them an idea of people who may think, dress, and act like you) and we check in when we are at locations to update our friends (this gives the restaurants, malls, and a host of other activities that you may be interested in).

As a result of this, our information has become big business, and this is why Facebook and many other services can afford to keep the site free for consumers or users. They make their money through targeted advertising and selling our information.

I am not saying Facebook is wrong or right for doing this. We do voluntarily give them this information, and often, targeted advertising helps us find great deals on products that we might not have otherwise encountered if this method of reaching customers did not exist. However, people have been fired for the content that they have on their Facebook accounts, and it is increasingly becoming something employers (to include the military) check before hiring a potential employee for activities or pictures deemed unacceptable.

Hence, this portion was intended to educate the reader on how his or her information is being used and how it can affect his or her overall lifestyle and opportunities.

## The Ugly

The credit bureau was meant to be a means of monitoring and measuring the creditworthiness of all our citizens. However, the three bureaus no longer have the public's best interest at heart as they are businesses for profit just like most other businesses in the United States. They offer a paid service of monitoring your credit, and in return, you are insured from fraudulent activity.

To ensure that they keep getting new customers, the credit bureaus intentionally leave inaccurate information on your report if you do not have the paid service. This is completely legal as they justify the inaccuracy as information that has been submitted about you by lending institutions and other business entities, which makes them blameless for errors on your report.

If you find the error on your free report and write to the credit bureau with supporting evidence, the bureau still has thirty days to respond to your claim and over sixty days to repair the damage. While you are waiting for the bureau to repair your credit score with the correct information, you will be unable to obtain favorable credit terms if able to receive credit at all.

The bureau will, at that time, offer to expedite the repair if you sign up for the paid service which is around $19 per month for the premium package, which is the one you will need to repair your credit in the desired time frame. This usually occurs when you are trying to apply for a mortgage or buy a new car. The reason for this occurring at the worst time possible is that they know that at that point you are desperate and will be more than willing to pay the fee of $19 to fix your report in order to get your house, your car, or even to maintain your security clearance for your job.

There is no incentive for changing this behavior as the government is aware of these actions being taken by the credit bureaus but is unable to change the laws without the Congress and Senate. Lobbyists (people paid by private corporations to speak to the government on a company's behalf) have infiltrated the system and pay a lot of money to keep the cycle going for a host of different companies, corporations, and special interests. These contributions are not given to the politicians for personal use. However, the money is donated in the form of campaign contributions, which are used to pay for the politicians' expenses when they make TV ads, posters, and need to pay for travel-related expenses to visit different cities to gain votes.

Just imagine if you were the credit bureau and you were making $19 per person each month for one year with approximately 30% (100 million people) of the US population signed up for your program. You would be making $1.9 billion per month (that is $22.8 billion each year).

If you are making that much money by keeping inaccurate records of information, what would be your incentive to change anything? Bad or incorrect information, as a result, has become big business for the credit bureaus, which creates a conflict of interest as their profits are literally linked to the companies performing mediocre or bad services to the end consumer (you).

This portion was not intended to incite hatred or disdain toward the credit bureaus, which can provide valuable services and benchmarks for consumer creditworthiness if governed correctly. This was merely an attempt to open the eyes of the reader to the role the credit bureaus currently play and how the system affects you as the consumer.

# How to Live in Excess and Afford It

As a nation, we are accustomed or used to having certain luxuries of life that we consider to be normal. We all want a big-screen TV, we all want to drive a nice car, and we all want the best for our children and grandchildren. However, we often don't make enough money to sustain the lifestyle we live.

As a result, we are trapped in a cycle of debt and have become used to carrying a balance on our credit cards, having a car payment, and having to pay for the convenience of having data capabilities on our smart cell phones. Because of this, we have developed many mechanisms in order to sustain our lofty lifestyles.

While trying to maintain this lifestyle of living above our means, many have fallen into financial difficulty or even attempted to take their own lives due to the mounting pressure of debt. This is all due to the perception that the consequence for having bad debt is worse than it really is.

The fact is that you can never be thrown in jail for having consumer debt. You can use the maximum amount of cash or credit available on all credit cards, and if you don't repay it, the worst that a credit card company can do is call you with harassing phone calls and make empty threats.

In order to stop these calls from the companies, you may file for bankruptcy. By law, the credit card companies can no longer contact you once you are in bankruptcy-protection status (filed for bankruptcy). There are a few debts that bankruptcy cannot get rid of such as student loans, governmental fees or fines, alimony or child support, lawsuit judgments, and condominium or association fees and assessments. Most other debts can be eliminated through filing bankruptcy (Attorney John Orcutt is a good place to start with no money down).

You may file what is known as a Chapter 7 bankruptcy or a Chapter 13 bankruptcy as an individual. Chapter 11 is usually reserved for businesses and corporations. With a Chapter 7 bankruptcy filing, you are telling creditors that you do not intend to repay the debt owed to them and you will be unable to receive any credit for two to seven years after your bankruptcy filing. In some cases, the time frame for creditworthiness does not start until the date the bankruptcy discharge is awarded by the court. This may be two to three years after you filed for the initial bankruptcy protection.

Chapter 13 is the most preferable form of bankruptcy as it tells the lender that you are willing to pay a portion of the debt back to them in small increments through the court or a trustee (person that acts as the middle man between you and the lender) using agreed-upon terms established by the Bankruptcy Court.

Chapter 13 is also the best form of bankruptcy to use if you are applying for or already have a security clearance, as it shows a willingness to accept responsibility for your actions or circumstances. Your financial situation may be due to divorce or some other life-changing event that affected your ability to meet your financial obligations in full for a short period of time.

This can be illustrated when you file a Chapter 13 as you will be forced to make scheduled on-time payments for a two-to-three-year period, which is enough time to assess whether you have an issue managing your finances or if it was an isolated incident.

Since you are already accustomed to living above your means, a good way to plan for how much you can charge on your credit card is to use your tax return to your advantage. If you make $40,000 per year and you have children, for example—you know you will receive the child tax credit and a few other things you can claim that cannot be disputed such as uniform, work, and mileage expenses; charitable donations in the form of drop-offs; energy-efficient additions to your home; and travel-related expenses.

Most of these do not require you to provide additional documentation and is almost impossible for the government to audit. Claiming these expenses on your tax return will get you a higher rate of return when you file your taxes.

If you average the amount of tax returns received for the past three years, you will be able to estimate what you will get the following year if your circumstances are relatively that same. If you deployed (soldiers), had a child, bought a car or bought a home, your tax return will be more for that year. Use this average of your past three years of returns and then divide it by twelve. This will give you the amount of additional income you are able to put on a credit card if you subtract the amount for the interest rate of the card.

If you make $40,000 per year and receive an average of $4,000 on your tax return, then you are able to spend $3,616 per month for the year adjusting $600 for the year in credit-card interest payment and fees. That is roughly an additional $282 that you can spend each month without actually falling into more debt.

This means you can get a car for a payment of $282 per month on a credit card with a limit of $3,500–$4,000 and have the government essentially pay for your vehicle every year without affecting your monthly or yearly salary. This formula works for all salary ranges and is based solely on the dollar amount of your average yearly tax return for the stated three-year period. Remember to always account for the interest rate of the credit card you use in order to obtain precise and accurate numbers.

Another form of obtaining additional income is to transfer the GI Bill benefits to your spouse. If your spouse enrolls in the recommended amount of classes to receive the maximum amount of benefits, you will receive a check every month that is intended to pay for school-related expenses. However, there is also additional money provided for books, room and board, and a host of other school-related expenses. This could easily add another $600–$1,350 per month to your yearly income. This would take you from the $43,316 per year (your $40,000 income combined with my tax formula above) to $50,816 on the low end and $59,516 on the high end.

Combining these two methods can supplement your income for a three-year period giving you an additional monthly salary amount of $1,626. This additional amount on top of your current salary is enough to take a three-year loan on a card and pay it off by paying $626 per month and afford an apartment lease or rental property for three years.

I do not recommend using this method for considering a home purchase as the GI Bill only lasts for thirty-six months (three years). This is enough time to pay off a car but will not work for a thirty-year mortgage payment. However, the tax formula method can be used to factor in the home purchase as you will receive your tax return

## VIRTUOUS CYCLE ECONOMICS

for the foreseeable future until a drastic change in lifestyle or the tax code occurs.

As a nation our problem has become the underlying inflation that is not being addressed, and therefore, coping mechanisms have to be used in order to maintain our way of life. An illustration of this inflation is, for example, in 1970 you paid $1 for a liter of coke and you were making $15 per hour, and today you are making $20 per hour but a liter of coke now cost $2. It means inflation doubled the price of the coke in a forty-four-year period, but your wage only increased by 33%. Over time, this disparity will only get wider if the trend continues.

Using that example, if inflation were to stay the same and the wage growth were to stay the same over the next forty-four years, taking us to 2058. A liter of coke will cost us $4.00, and your wage will only be $26.60 per hour, which is a $6.60 increase per hour in forty-four years. This means your wage would have only increased by $0.0125 per year for that time period.

This is the reality of how our economy has stagnated. If you actually knew that you would only receive a raise of one penny per year for the next forty-four years, would you still work for that company or corporation? This is the nature of the minimum wage system in our country, and it is only a matter of time before it starts eroding the free market as 70% of our market depends on those consumers and their discretionary spending.

This was intended to educate the reader on ways to cope with debt and explore different options available to provide planned and sustained means of supplemental income. If you are a middle-class citizen ($25,000–$75,000 per year), then the odds of upward mobility is stacked against you as 42% of the population born in poverty will stay in poverty for the duration of their lifetime (accounting for inflation).

# Your Security Clearance and Your Finances

Your ability to obtain a security clearance and your finances are closely linked. The reason for this is that your ability to repay your debts is an indication of your overall frame of mind and the ability for you to fall prey to certain situations or circumstance. For example, if you have a lot of debt and have access to valuable information, you may be tempted to sell this information in the eyes of the security clearance issuer and be deemed a security risk. This could cause you to lose your security clearance or be downgraded to a lesser role or clearance level.

It has been true throughout our history that most traitors have leaked information to third parties for financial gain because they were driven by mounting debts or mediocre life circumstances and wanted to quickly achieve some upward mobility (get rich).

However, if you do fall into financial difficulty while having a secret or top secret clearance, there are steps you can take to keep your clearance. If you find yourself in a position where you need some financial relief, talk to the issuing authority for your security clearance (if military, the S2 shop) and get advice on steps to take to avoid losing your clearance. If you need to file a bankruptcy, a Chapter 13 is the best option that allows you to work with your creditors and provide documentation to the issuing authority for your security clearance that you are not a security risk.

This was intended to give a snap shot of how your finances may affect your security clearance and how to address this issue if it arises.

# Cash Only?

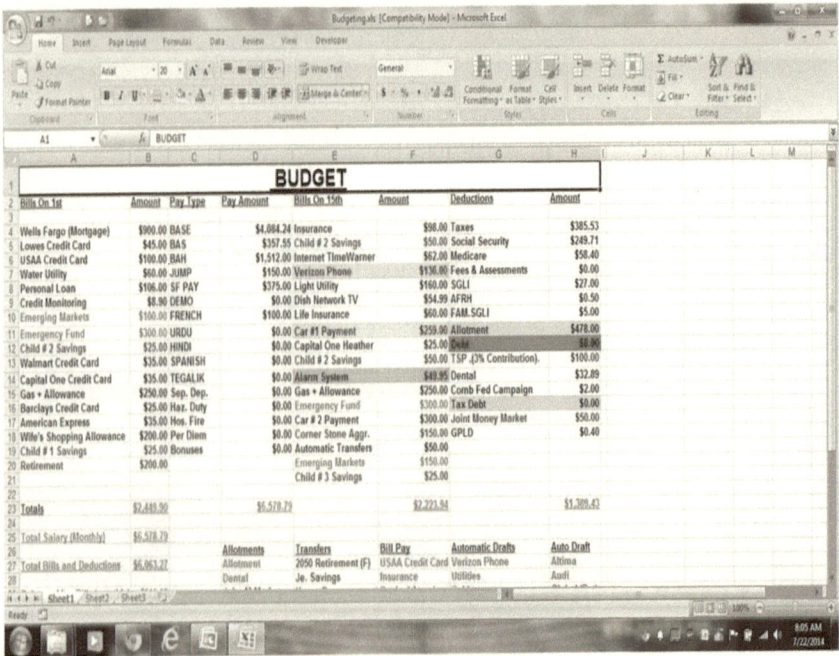

As a society today the concept of living on cash only is almost an oxymoron (self-defeating statement or action). We can hardly imagine ourselves living by using only cash as a method of payment. Cash is not a viable option for some situations including purchasing a home, buying a nice car, paying for college, and so on. These large

## VIRTUOUS CYCLE ECONOMICS

purchases usually have to be financed in order for the everyday consumer to be able to afford them.

However, if you file for bankruptcy, you will be faced with this harsh reality. After filing for bankruptcy, regardless of whether you file for a Chapter 11 or Chapter 13, you will be prohibited from borrowing or having any credit cards. Banks will no longer grant you a loan, and you will be forced use cash only for a period of roughly two years.

After filing for a bankruptcy, you can be allowed to be placed on your spouse's or parents' credit cards as an authorized user. This will lend their credit history to you and positively affect your credit score if their payments have been on time for the account to which you have been added. You can ask your parents, friends, or significant others to do this to help you rebuild your credit and to have a credit card to use while you go through the bankruptcy process.

If they are unwilling to add you as an authorized user with a card due to trust issues, you can have them authorize you as a user but not possess a card. This way you still get the credit score benefit of being on an account in good standing in preparation for the end of you bankruptcy period.

If you get someone to do this for you during your bankruptcy period, you will have a good credit rating when you bankruptcy is discharged. This will occur for a few reasons. You will be debt free for the most part, the financial institutions know that you have been forced to become more disciplined with your finance, and they also know that you are more likely to use credit and carry a balance.

You will start receiving multiple offers for credit cards after your bankruptcy discharge because of this and you must be careful in selecting the right types of cards. Your new credit score will qualify you for better rates of interest than you previously had before. Look for credit card offers with no annual fee (not only promotional), no black-out dates for using reward points, try to get cards with interest rates at the prime rate (rate that is industry minimum being charged by all credit issuers). Prime rate plus 1–4% is acceptable. For example, an interest rate of 9.9% is not uncommon for a person with good credit. With excellent credit, however, one may qualify for 0–5% interest rates.

Even if you are not in a financial hardship situation, you can still use the accounts of others (friends, family, or spouse) in order to improve your credit rating and receive lower interest rates using the method previously stated herein. Another way to save on interest rate payment is to apply jointly with your spouse or parent for loans if their credit is in good standing and they are willing to help. You must, however, ensure that your payments are made on time as this will affect their credit and make them liable for the debt if you do not pay on time or refuse to pay back the debt.

This was meant to educate the readers on some options available if faced with a situation where you may be forced to live on cash only, such as the period following a bankruptcy filing. This was in no way intended to promote any perversion of the system or promote fraudulent activity.

# Budgeting

Budgeting has been around for ages and is one of the hardest things for a young person to follow. However, budgeting is a necessary part of life and can be made easy if the correct steps are taken.

One way to make a budget that works and one that is efficient is to first assess your income and compare it to your bills by using a Microsoft Excel worksheet (provided with this book). The worksheet is formulated to automatically calculate the figures you enter into each column. The description of the items can be edited, but the color codes should be strictly followed. The red color is for debts, the blue color is for savings and investment accounts, and the green column is for money coming in or money remaining after all bills have been paid in full on a monthly payment basis.

After filling in the worksheet, take a look at bills that are just wants and things that you may be able to trim down or cut out all together. Cable companies, phone service providers, credit card companies, banks, and most consumer-lending organizations are usually willing to lower your bill if you either threaten to leave or simply explain that you will no longer be able to afford their service at the current price due to a change in your financial circumstances. You can often save about $100 per in total per month and pay less than what you are paying currently by just making a few phone calls to these providers.

The next step is to put all your bills on auto bill pay. You now know exactly how much money is coming in and how much is going out, and you are now able to account for your additional income as explained earlier in this book (tax return + GI bill benefits).

Many companies offer an additional savings on your interest rate if you agree to set up automatic payments. This can save you 0.25% on most of your accounts which adds up over time (USAA offers this for all loans if you set up automatic payments). USAA also offers up to $900 in cash back if you purchase a home using an agent from the USAA home buyers program. Even if you don't use USAA as your mortgage provider, they will still pay you the funds as long as you use a USAA affiliated realtor. (Shawn and Kevin Grullon from Coldwell Banker is a good place to start at 910-257-3027.)

Refinancing your loans at lower interest rates may also save you some money if you add a spouse with good credit, or if your credit score has improved since you were first extended credit. If you are in the military, you should always use the VA loan option. This will ensure that you save $150–$250 in mortgage insurance premium known as PMI (primary mortgage insurance), which you will have to pay when you use a conventional loan and do not have the required 20% down payment available. You will be required to pay this amount in addition to your mortgage payment, which will be paid through an Escrow account until you have paid your mortgage down to having at least that 20% equity in the property. (Equity is the amount of money you owe on your mortgage minus the amount your home is currently worth on the real estate market.)

Make sure that you calculate how much money refinancing will cost you in the long run and if you are actually saving money. Also

## VIRTUOUS CYCLE ECONOMICS

keep in mind your goal of refinancing. If you want to get a lower monthly payment in order to have more free cash flow at the end of each month, and you are young enough (under thirty-five years old), then it may be a good option for you to cash out and take some money out of your house. You may also borrow against the equity in your car or motorcycle. If you paid a big down payment on your vehicle, or your vehicle just simply holds it value, you may be able to tap into the equity through your financial institution by cashing out and also receiving a lower interest rate.

However, when you receive these large amounts of windfalls (reenlistment bonuses or holiday bonuses), it is important not to just blow the money on consumer items. Ensure there is a plan in place for this money and try to make that money work for you in order to make more money.

This was intended to give the reader a variety of options in which to establish a budget, find alternate sources of acquiring additional funds, and lowering overall monthly expenditures (bills) by making a few simple phone calls. A CD is enclosed with the budgeting tool. Follow the attached instructions and you will be well on your way to a sound financial standing and a bright future.

# Investing for Beginners

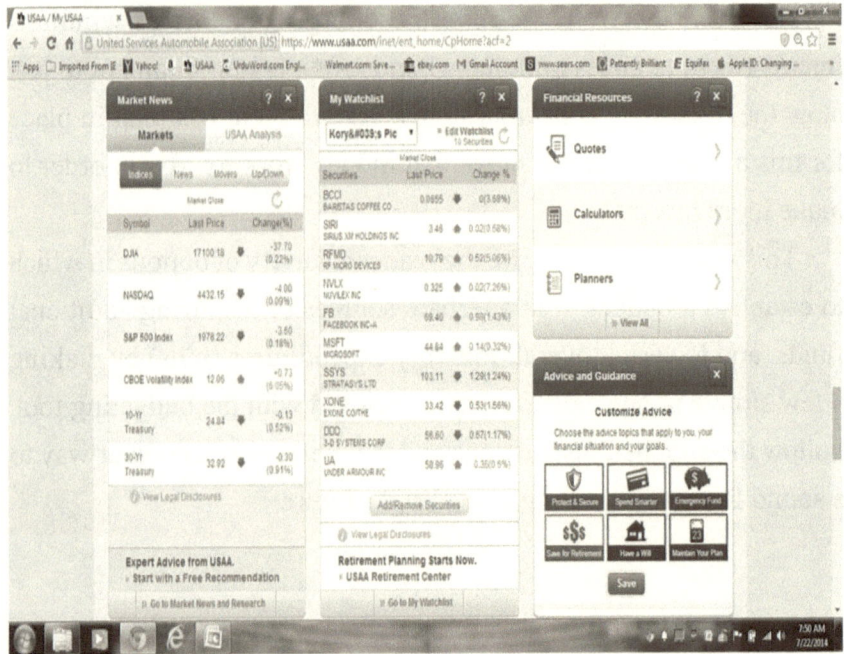

The stock market can be a complicated place to put your money, or at least so it may seem at first glance. However, the stock market is one of the safest places for your money to be to earn a decent rate of return and have a nest egg for retirement.

Most Americans see Wall Street as a corrupt place, and see the bankers and hedge fund managers as monsters. With movies like

## VIRTUOUS CYCLE ECONOMICS

*The Wolf of Wall Street* out there for all to see combined with the hype of media and propaganda, Wall Street has been given a bad rap. However, if you understand how the market works, you can make the market work for you just like it does for millionaires and billionaires.

Take for example the enlistment and reenlistment bonuses the army pays its soldiers. The average amount ranges from around $10,000 to $30,000 for most military occupational specialties (MOS) and is upward of $50,000 for some specialized areas. If you were to invest that $50,000 into a fund that yields an average of 8% compounded interest per year for twenty years without withdrawing the funds, you turn that $50,000 into $566,666. That is over a half of a million dollars by letting it sit in that account for the duration of a twenty-year military career if you received that bonus when you first enlisted. For the $10,000 amount, you would see a return of $113,333 in twenty years.

However, as we know, you receive more than one bonus throughout your military career; and you will also receive additional funds during deployments. If these additional funds are set aside and invested properly, you can easily retire from the military as a millionaire. If you can turn that initial $10,000 into $113,333, you can turn that extra $10,000–$30,000 you may save during deployments and have the same multiples.

You will also receive reenlistment bonuses that should be set aside in the same manner. This is assuming you go with the funds that have that compounded annual rate of return. However, there are more aggressive avenues that can earn you 39% instead of 8% on your money. Those funds generally have a high upside and a pretty large downside as well if they don't perform. In other words, the more risky a fund is, you can make up to 39% on your money or lose 25% of your money in the same time period. This is why you should take the steady moderately aggressive funds that are a mixture of stocks and government-held bonds. Bonds are generally considered safe and are guaranteed or insured by the government, but usually have a low set rate of return on your investment.

In order to really make your money work in the stock market as an average investor just starting out, you need to understand some key portions of the market and ignore the noise. There are a lot of confusing words and terms used to make the market sound complicated, so you may feel intimidated or think there is no way you can understand the market and how it works.

However, these were put in place by Wall Street fat cats and brokers (people who trade stock on your behalf) in order to make themselves more important and remain relevant so they can keep charging you money to do what you can already do for yourself but are too intimidated or afraid to make a mistake.

A few simple steps to get you started in knowing the difference in the type of stock in which to invest to make the most of your money. First, write down some well-known companies and then research their stock price by going to the Yahoo website and clicking on the header that says Finance. This will give you a snap shot of the market and will give you a search box in which you can type the names of companies. Type these companies in the search box so you may see the value or stock price of that company today at this very moment in time as this is a delayed feed that is pretty much updated every few seconds. Look up the following companies: Amazon, Google, Yahoo, and Facebook. These companies are well-known and have established relatively high stock prices for the everyday investor. They are in the $30–$600 range which are established and relatively stable stocks.

**VIRTUOUS CYCLE ECONOMICS**

The other stocks on the other end of the spectrum are the most profitable, but also the most volatile (swing up and down drastically). These are called penny stocks which will range from fractions of a penny to around $4. These stocks can rise 1,000% and make you a lot of money within hours. However, they can also lose 1,000% in a few hours or even seconds for no other reason than investor sentiment (how an investor feels or guesses that the stock is going to perform). These are usually start-up companies that are looking for money to get their businesses off the ground level and are in a critical stage where they may make it big or fail.

If you get in on the ground level of one of these companies, you can become a millionaire in a matter of months. However, this method of investing takes a lot of luck and understanding what the market is doing relative to the actual performance of the company, investors that are placing bets on that company to fail (commonly known as a short or shorting the stock) that will all factor into how the stock price fluctuates. If you put your $10,000 in a stock the cost of a penny ($0.01) per share, you would receive one million shares of that company. If that stock goes up to being worth $1 per share you would become a millionaire that day as your one million shares would now be worth $1 million at $1 per share. If it goes to being worth $10 per share, you would see your initial $10,000 investment become $10 million. However, you can just as quickly and easily lose all your money.

This happens all the time on Wall Street, but the problem is that you have to be able to find that diamond in the rough and get really lucky to find that great pick and have the courage and discipline to ride the price from $0.01 per share to $10 per share.

Instead of doing this and gambling with your money, I suggest finding what are termed as midcap stocks. These are stocks that are over the $4-per-share range but under the $10–$15 price range. These stocks are usually stocks that have been proven to last beyond the penny stock stage and are poised to explode into the high valuations of say Amazon or Google if they are handled correctly by their respective corporations. In my opinion, this is the safest route to invest your hard-earned money without dealing with the high volatility of penny stocks and without being able to afford a share of Google for $580 per share.

However, I would not recommend just jumping into the market with your hard-earned money without first testing the waters as a beginner. My suggestion is to first write down the companies in the midcap range that pique your interest and use play or fake money to just buy them on paper. After you pick your fake investments, you should track the progress of those stocks you bought with pretend money and see where you would be if you had invested your real money in the market. This way you get to track your progress and see how the market performs without the risk of losing your real money.

You can find all this information about a company when you follow the search method mentioned earlier on by going to Yahoo and clicking on the Finance tab. You will then see the Quote Lookup search area on the left side of the page. After entering the name of the company or its stock symbol, the company's current stock price and the day's performance will populate on the page.

You should then look on the left side where you will see the summary, charts, news, and information highlighted in black, and then the portion that reads Company. Under this heading, you will be able to select Key Statistics. This is where you will find all the important information I suggested reviewing before making a decision on a company.

You should also pay particular attention to how long the company has been in business, how relevant is the product or service they provide, is their product patented and exclusive to just that company, the amount of debt the company has, and the amount of money the company makes currently each quarter (every three months).

You should also pay attention to how many insiders (people who work at the company) are holding on to shares of the stock, the fifty-two-week low and high of the stock (the lowest and highest price over a one year period) and the EBITDA (earnings before interest, taxes, depreciation, and amortizations). This will give you a good indication of where the company is heading financially. Even if a company has an outstanding product, they could go bankrupt if is not managed well and is operating in the negatives (RED) for an extended period of time.

Keep in mind that most companies lose money during their first years of operation. The key thing to take away is the amount of debt the company has and the amount of money the company is making each quarter (every three months). If the company owes $10 million to the bank but is making $5 million every quarter on its books, then you can assume that the company will be able to pay off its debt and become profitable within a reasonable timeframe.

Using this information, you will be able to take a lot of the guess work out of investing and simply go with a solid company with good fundamentals. It is also important to note that you should invest whenever you can in the companies you select whether the price is high or low. This will give you what is known as averaging which allows you not to have to time the market in order to get good deals. If the company is a good company, then any fair price is a good deal.

After you have decided that you are comfortable with your results, it is now time to set up a stock brokerage account with a brokerage company (E-trade) or a financial institution that doesn't operate on commission, such as USAA whose brokers operate on a salary. There will still be fees associated with trading, but they are much lower than going with conventional stock brokers who charge high fees in order to stuff their pockets and have no vested interest in if you make money or lose money as they still collect on your trade no matter what.

USAA has low fees and reduces the fees the more often you trade. You are able to go from different levels of trading depending on how frequently you trade. A platinum-level trader might pay $5 per trade in its entirety while a gold-level trader may pay $8 per trade for the same exact transaction and dollar amount. (Fees per trade are not per stock but for the whole transaction; whether I trade one hundred shares or three hundred shares, I will still be paying the same flat $5 or $8.) This method is set up in different levels, however, as you have different thresholds that require a higher fee. For example, if you trade above two thousand shares, then you may pay $10 for the transaction instead of the $5 to $8 price tag. See the rules of your financial institution, or call and simply say, "Set up a brokerage account," to get the information from the institution. The information is completely free.

When everyone else gets scared or worried when the market starts to turn downward, this is the time to buy more of your stock and you should consider it, as you would, a *sale* at your local convenience store. You would normally buy more of something you like at the grocery store if it is offered at a discounted rate no matter what other people thought of that product. The same principles should apply to your investments. This is how you beat the market at its own game. Make steady investments in a solid stock over time and you will be able to retire comfortably. The famous Oracle of Omaha, Mr. Warren

Buffet, one of the most well-known and respected minds in the investment business, said it best when he stated, "Be fearful when others are greedy and be greedy when others are fearful."

This was intended to provide a base-level understanding of the stock market for an investor in the beginning stages. It was also intended to provide financial advice on different methods of making today's stock market work for the average investor seeking to make steady gains over time in preparation for a fruitful retirement. The army's thrift savings plan is also an option for soldiers to utilize. With the thrift savings plan, you are able to choose whether you want to manage your own funds by allocating them where you see fit, or you can have your money automatically invested for you. Using the automatic method is recommended if you do not thoroughly understand the market.

# Wealth Management

After you have followed the investment advice in the previous chapters, and you have now struck it rich, this advice will save you a sizable amount of money. If you have made $1 million within a year, you are now considered to be in the top 1% of earners in the United States and must now learn how the rich protect their money now that you fall into that category.

First you must avoid the high income tax rate of 35% by allowing your assets to be claimed as capital gains which most investment profits fall under for which the tax rate is currently 15%. This will save you 20% of your earnings, and you will only pay $150,000 in taxes instead of $350,000, which is a savings of $200,000 for the year.

You can also reduce your salary to $1 for the year if you decide to form a business and make another $2 million. You can take your paycheck in the form of stock options which can only be taxed as capital gains at the lower 15% again instead of 35%. This will allow your $1 per year salary to be taxed only 35¢ (yes, 35¢) for the entire year. You will pay the 15% capital gains tax on your additional $2 million in stock options and pay only $300,000 instead of $700,000 if you were to take the money as income instead of stock options. This is a method used by Facebook's founder in order to lower his taxable income.

**VIRTUOUS CYCLE ECONOMICS**

You can also research setting up a trust and gifting up to $12,000 per year to family members without incurring taxes on the amount. There are numerous ways to take advantage of the current tax code if you become wealthy. However, these options are not available if you don't have the money and fall between the $25,000–$75,000 middle-class range. You will be stuck paying the full 33%–35% on average with no wiggle room whatsoever.

This was intended to provide information on how to avoid high taxes on amassed wealth and does not in any way endorse or support these methods of avoiding one's patriotic duty to pay our fair share of taxes as upstanding American citizens. It was merely meant to illustrate the options available to the reader if and when he or she were to obtain a certain financial status.

I hope you have learned something from reading what I have written, and I wish you all the best in your future endeavors. Out of many, we are one people. God bless you, and God bless America—the best nation on earth!

# About the Author

I was born in St. Thomas, Jamaica, in the Princess Margaret Hospital on the thirteenth day of November 1981 (it was a Friday). My father was a chef working for the United States Navy in Guantanamo Bay (Cuba), and my mother was an early-education schoolteacher.

I was taught to read at an early age by my mother, and I read books such as *Emil and the Detectives*, *The Young Warriors*, *The Cloud with the Silver Lining*, and *Oliver Twist*. My early childhood and middle school education took place in Jamaica; but at the age of fourteen, in 1998, we migrated to the United States of America.

I had always dreamed of coming to America, and it somehow felt more like home to me than anywhere else I had ever been. I had always heard the term *land of opportunity* and believed in this ideal wholeheartedly.

I and my older brother Greg excelled at academics while attending North East High School in Saint Petersburg, Florida. However, shortly after my fifteenth birthday, I obtained a job working at the local Winn-Dixie as a stocker, and my grades began to suffer a bit.

This was my first job, and it lasted only for a few months. This was as a result of accidentally being thrown from a ladder when the store manager bumped into it while I was still at the top attempting to retrieve items to restock the store shelves.

I injured my shoulder, and my mother decided it was best for me to terminate my employment with Winn-Dixie. Shortly after leaving Winn-Dixie, I went to work for the Publix grocery chain bagging groceries.

At this time in my life, I was in love with the sport of soccer, and my brother and I decided to try out for the North East High School soccer team (the Vikings). We were unsuccessful in our attempt to make the team, and it was a difficult reality to accept.

My brother then decided to focus exclusively on his academics and gave up the dream of playing soccer. However, it was extremely difficult for me to accept this failure. Hence, after soccer tryouts, I immediately went home and started practicing in order to ensure that I would make the team the following year.

I practiced every day from the day I got told I wasn't good enough to make the team until the next year when I again attended the team tryouts. I practiced without regard for weather, time of day, or physical pain. I had to make the team—and make the team I did.

I was voted one of the three team captains on the North East High School soccer team in 1999. It was one of the proudest moments of my entire life. It was extremely gratifying due to the hard work that I had put in to ensuring that I gave myself the best chance I could to be selected as a member of the squad.

Later that year, the path of my life was altered when an army sergeant (recruiter) visited our home in order to convince my brother to sign up for military service. As we were sitting at the table listening to the recruiter, it was I who became more interested in joining the service.

My mother was completely against this decision; and since I was only seventeen years old at the time, I could not sign up without my parents' consent (as I was not yet eighteen years of age) and would require a signed waiver. I was determined to join the service and therefore asked my father to sign the document.

He consulted with my mother and convinced her to sign the document since I felt so strongly about it. I was only 150 pounds soaking wet, and my father saw me as feeble and sickly as in my earlier years I frequently visited the doctor for common afflictions such as a cold and various allergies.

His decision was based on the fact that he thought I would attend the army's boot camp training and fail to meet the standards. I would then return home realizing my mistake and continue on the path they had envisioned for me.

He could not have been more wrong. I applied myself with the same determination that I had with my soccer regimen; and despite starting in the bottom 10% of the physically fit candidates when we began the training, I emerged in the end as top of my graduating class.

I received an Army Achievement Medal for physical fitness and was promoted to the next higher rank of PV2 at my graduation ceremony. I was one of three soldiers of a class of three hundred selected to represent the graduating class at the front of the formation, and I accepted my bestowed honor with the utmost pride.

Upon graduating the basic training course, I was sent to complete my military occupational specialty (MOS) training as a power-generator technician for a period of five months in Aberdeen (Maryland). After successfully completing the training, I was then sent overseas to my first duty station in Hanau, Germany.

I then saw my first deployment to Kosovo within my first few months at my new base camp. It was here that I met an army captain; and again, it would alter the course of my life. He was a Green Beret (Special Forces soldier), and he carried himself in such a way that he stood out from the rest of us. I was so impressed by his demeanor and professionalism that I felt compelled to talk to him even though I was only a private. (This is the equivalent of a factory assembly-line worker walking up to the CEO and asking him how he did it.)

The captain spoke to me as if I were an equal and answered all my questions. It was then that I decided that one day I wanted to be like him; I wanted to be a Green Beret.

Shortly after leaving Kosovo, I deployed to Poland for the Joint Visitors Bureau (JVB) where I was one of the few soldiers selected as a part of a detail (a group of tasked soldiers) to drive for General Wallace, General Myers, and General Shinseki.

Shortly after the (JVB) deployment, the September 11 events occurred, and I found myself in Iraq soon thereafter. Upon completing my Iraq tour, my four-year contract had ended and my first child was on its way. I then decided it was time to use the Montgomery GI Bill to attend school in order to obtain a college degree.

While attending college in Saint Petersburg, I chose to pursue a degree in criminal justice as I intended on becoming a police officer. However, after receiving three speeding tickets within a two-year period while in the program, I was not permitted to advance to the schoolhouse (residency) phase of the police academy.

As a result, I reentered active military service in March of 2006 and signed a contract to train as an aviation electrician (MOS 15F). While serving as an aviation electrician in Fort Riley (Kansas), I had a chance encounter with a Special Forces recruiter and decided that it was time to pursue my dream job.

I then attended the Special Forces Assessment and Selection course in Fort Bragg (North Carolina) and successfully completed the training. I was selected to attend the second phase of the course as a satellite communications sergeant (MOS 18E). I successfully completed the training in 2009 and joined the Special Forces Regiment. It was one of the proudest moments of my life, and one of my greatest achievements that my family can be proud of for generations to come.

Currently, I am in my fourteenth year of service, and I can now proudly add *author* and *inventor* to my list of accomplishments. I am married to my wife of seven years, Heather, and I have three beautiful children: Jalen, Jenai, and Justin. I have recently made the distinction between the man I really am and the man that *God* intended me to be. I have recently made changes in my life in order to move closer to God, and I thank you for purchasing my book and for visiting this website. May God bless you, and may God bless America, the greatest nation on earth.

www.ingramcontent.com/pod-product-compliance
Lightning Source LLC
Chambersburg PA
CBHW021044180526
45163CB00005B/2270